Sports
Illustrated
KI

STARS OF SPORTS

SUNI
LEE

GYMNASTICS SUPERSTAR

■ ■ ▌ by Cheryl Kim

CAPSTONE PRESS
a capstone imprint

Published by Capstone Press, an imprint of Capstone
1710 Roe Crest Drive, North Mankato, Minnesota 56003
capstonepub.com

Library of Congress Cataloging-in-Publication Data
Names: Kim, Cheryl, author.
Title: Suni Lee : gymnastics superstar / by Cheryl Kim.
Description: North Mankato, Minnesota : Capstone Press, 2023. | Series: Stars of sports | "Sports Illustrated Kids." | Includes bibliographical references and index. | Audience: Ages 8 to 11 | Audience: Grades 4-6 | Summary: "Readers learn about Suni Lee's, childhood, young gymnastics career, and road to the Olympics"— Provided by publisher.
Identifiers: LCCN 2022047870 (print) | LCCN 2022047871 (ebook) | ISBN 9781669018124 (hardcover) | ISBN 9781669018070 (paperback) | ISBN 9781669018087 (pdf) | ISBN 9781669018100 (kindle edition) | ISBN 9781669018117 (epub)
Subjects: LCSH: Lee, Sunisa, 2003- —Juvenile literature. | Women gymnasts—United States—Biography—Juvenile literature. | Women Olympic athletes—United States—Biography—Juvenile literature. | Hmong American women—Biography—Juvenile literature.
Classification: LCC GV460.2.L44 K56 2023 (print) | LCC GV460.2.L44 (ebook) | DDC 796.44092 [B]—dc23/eng/20221128
LC record available at https://lccn.loc.gov/2022047870
LC ebook record available at https://lccn.loc.gov/2022047871

Editorial Credits
Editor: Mandy Robbins; Designer: Hilary Wacholz; Media Researcher: Jo Miller; Production Specialist: Tori Abraham

Source Notes
Pg. 8, "If I wasn't in the gym . . ." "Suni Lee's Dad Built Her A Beam So She Could Practice In Her Backyard As A Kid," *Romper*, by Jen McGuire, July 30, 2021, https://www.romper.com/life/suni-lee-dad-built-beam-backyard
Pg. 14, "I ended up . . . " "Injuries. Trolls. Her own nerves. Gymnast Sunisa Lee battles them all in Olympic quest," MPR News, by Nancy Yang, March 20, 2020, https://www.mprnews.org/story/2020/03/20/injuries-trolls-her-own-nerves-gymnast-sunisa-lee-battles-them-all-in-olympic-quest
Pg. 16, "There were a lot of times . . . " "How Sunisa Lee overcame family tragedy and injury to win Olympic gold," *The Guardian*, by Joan Niesen, July 30, 2021, https://www.theguardian.com/sport/2021/jul/30/sunisa-lee-gymnastics-gold-hmong-americans-olympics
Pg. 17, "My community supports me . . . " "Sunisa Lee reflects on recent success, while looking ahead to possible Olympic run," MPR News, by Simone Cazares, August 14, 2019, https://www.mprnews.org/story/2019/08/14/sunisa-lee-reflects-on-recent-success-while-looking-ahead-to-possible-olympic-run
Pg. 20, "This medal means . . . " "THE 100 MOST INFLUENTIAL PEOPLE OF 2021: Sunisa Lee," *TIME* magazine, by Nastia Luikin, September 9, 2021, https://time.com/collection/100-most-influential-people-2021/6095814/sunisa-lee/
Pg. 22, "I really just wanted to come . . . " "A look at life after gold for Olympic medalist Suni Lee," 11Alive, by Maria Martin, February 15, 2022, https://www.11alive.com/article/sports/olympics/2020-tokyo-olympics-gold-medal-gymnast-suni-lee-auburn-university/85-d02c4b51-062e-43a7-8487-90e3293bc819
Pg. 24, "When you're an elite gymnast . . ." "From gold to orange and blue: Olympian Sunisa Lee enters new routine as star student," The Newsroom: The Official Source for Auburn University News, by Preston Sparks, September 29, 2021, https://ocm.auburn.edu/newsroom/news_articles/2021/09/091425-suni-lee.php
Pg. 28, "Suni has an impact . . ." "THE 100 MOST INFLUENTIAL PEOPLE OF 2021: Sunisa Lee," *TIME* magazine, by Nastia Luikin, September 9, 2021, https://time.com/collection/100-most-influential-people-2021/6095814/sunisa-lee/

All internet sites appearing in back matter were available and accurate when this book was sent to press.

TABLE OF CONTENTS

Words in **BOLD** are in the glossary.

A GOLDEN MOMENT

Suni Lee took a deep breath before beginning her final routine. She was competing in the Women's all-around competition at the Tokyo Olympic Games in 2021. She positioned herself in the corner of the floor. The music started. Lee powered ahead before leaping into a roundoff and back **handspring**. Her hands shot up as she landed upright. She completed her most difficult floor skill flawlessly!

Lee gracefully tiptoed and turned around for the double layout back handspring. She flipped her straightened body into the air twice and finished with a strong landing. The crowd cheered. Lee prepared for her final tumbling pass. She kept her focus and sprung into a back one-and-a-half and front full flip.

The music ended. Lee clapped her hands together. She hugged her coach as she waited for her score. The screen flashed 13.700. Lee took the lead for the all-around gold.

>>> Suni Lee performs her floor routine during the Tokyo Olympic Games in 2021.

CHAPTER ONE

A LOVE OF GYMNASTICS

Sunisa "Suni" Lee was born on March 9, 2003, in St. Paul, Minnesota. Lee's mother, Yeev, met John Lee, when Suni was 2 years old. Both John and Yeev came to the United States from Laos as young **refugees**. Legally, John is Lee's stepfather, but she considers him her father. Lee grew up with two older stepsiblings and three younger half-siblings.

Lee loved gymnastics from a young age. She jumped on the bed and did backflips. She tumbled across the living room. She swung from the metal bars on the clothesline in her backyard. Her parents contacted their friend Puner Koy who coached gymnastics nearby. He watched 6-year-old Lee. He advised her parents to let her train at Midwest Gymnastics in Little Canada, Minnesota. Owner Jess Graba also noticed her talent. He placed Lee in the fast-track program.

>>> Coach Jess Graba watches Suni Lee at practice in 2017.

Lee began training at the Midwest Gymnastics center. She practiced a lot on the beam. Her father couldn't afford to buy one for her to use at home. Instead, he made one using wood from an old mattress. After coming home from the gym, Lee practiced more on the beam in her backyard. "If I wasn't in the gym, I was always outside on the beam doing extra things because I didn't want to get behind or I always wanted to get better," said Lee.

There are 10 levels in the USA Gymnastics Junior Olympic program. To pass a level, gymnasts must master specific skills. At 8 years old, Lee jumped up three levels in just one year.

FACT

At 7 years old, Lee won the all-around competition at a state meet.

At 9 years old, Lee performed a **front aerial** to back handspring stepout on the high beam. Gold medalist Gabby Douglas did the same move in the 2012 London Olympics.

⟩⟩⟩ Suni Lee doing core exercises. A strong core is necessary in gymnastics.

CHAPTER TWO

AN ELITE GYMNAST

By age 12, Lee joined the sub-**elite** HOPES level of the Junior Olympic program. She won the 2015 HOPES Championship in Chicago. The following year, Lee reached the highest level of the Junior Olympic program. She became a junior elite gymnast. Elite gymnasts are the best in the world. Lee trained 36 to 38 hours a week.

Lee made her elite **debut** at the U.S. Classic in 2016. Every summer, elite artistic gymnasts from across the United States compete in the meet. Lee placed 16th in the all-around. Two years later, she placed 5th in the all-around. She also won gold on the balance beam and bronze on the uneven bars.

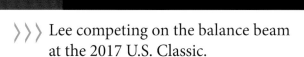

〉〉〉 Lee competing on the balance beam at the 2017 U.S. Classic.

In 2017, Lee received an invitation to attend the USA Gymnastics National Team Camp. During the camp, gymnasts are tested on their physical abilities. Lee impressed the judges. They invited her to join the U.S. National Team. There were only 28 teens from across the country on the team.

A month later, Lee joined a team of four U.S. gymnasts to compete in the Gymnix International Cup in Canada. Although she fell on the uneven bars, she won silver for the vault, balance beam, and floor routine. Her team won the junior division title. Sadly, Lee injured her ankle shortly afterward. She had to withdraw from a later international competition.

FACT

Out of millions of gymnasts in the United States, only about 80 women and 130 men make it to the elite level. Junior Elite gymnasts are 11 to 15 years old. Senior Elite gymnasts are 16 and up.

In 2018, Lee competed at the U.S. National Championship. She placed first in the uneven bars and second in the balance beam for the junior division. At the U.S. Classic, Lee took fifth in the all-around and gold on the balance beam in the junior division.

Lee performs her floor routine at the 2018 U.S. Classic.

CHAPTER THREE

PATH TO THE OLYMPICS

In 2019, just days before the U.S. National Championships, Lee's father fell from a ladder. The fall left him **paralyzed** from the chest down.

Lee wanted to skip the competition to be with her father. She visited him before his surgery. He encouraged her to still compete. Lee decided to remain in the National Championships. "I ended up pulling myself together and switching gears and competing for my dad," she said.

Lee's decision paid off. She placed first in the uneven bars and third in the floor routine. In the all-around, she placed second, just behind 2016 Olympic gold medal winner Simone Biles.

The U.S. Gymnastics Committee selected Lee to compete on the U.S. team at the 2019 World Championships in Stuttgart, Germany. There, Lee won silver for her floor routine and bronze for the uneven bars. USA Gymnastics won their fifth straight word title!

〉〉〉 Lee (left) on the podium receiving silver in the floor routine, next to Simone Biles with the gold and Russia's Angelina Melnikova, who took bronze.

Lee went on to compete in the U.S. Olympic trials. She placed second, earning a spot on the U.S. Olympic team. She would be the first Hmong-American Olympian to ever compete in the games. But the 2020 Tokyo Summer Olympics were postponed because of **COVID-19**. Lee's gym also closed because of the pandemic. When Lee returned to the gym to train, she injured her ankle. She couldn't practice for three months. "There were a lot of time[s] I wanted to quit," says Lee. But she didn't give up.

〉〉〉 Lee stretches in the gym wearing a medical boot on her injured ankle.

>>> Lee's family and Hmong community members came together to watch Lee compete in the Olympics.

A Community Behind Her

Suni Lee made history as the first Hmong-American Olympian. The Hmong are an ethnic group from Southeast Asia. They do not have their own country. Most live in Laos, Vietnam, and China. They helped the United States during the Vietnam War (1955–1975). To thank them, the United States allowed some families to **immigrate** to the United States.

Lee often speaks about the close community she grew up in. During her training years, they held fundraisers to support her. When she competed in the Olympics, more than 300 people from her community gathered with her family to cheer her on. "My community supports me a lot," says Lee. "I don't want to let them down, so I go out and compete for them."

CHAPTER FOUR

OLYMPIC CHAMPION

At the Tokyo Olympics, many people expected Simone Biles to win the gold medal. Biles ended up withdrawing from the all-around events for mental health reasons. Lee was ranked just behind Biles.

Lee suddenly found herself in the spotlight. She started with the vault. She received a solid score of 14.6. Next, Lee hit the uneven bars. She nailed a routine that was more difficult than those of her competitors. On the beam, Lee wobbled after a tricky triple turn. But she stayed on. She dismounted with two back handsprings and a double-twist and stuck the landing!

Her final event was the floor routine. In second place, Lee needed a score of 13.466 to take the lead. She scored 13.700 with one gymnast left to perform. Lee watched on as Brazil's Rebeca Andrade took the floor. Andrade stepped out of bounds twice. Lee won the gold medal!

>>> Lee performing her beam routine at the Tokyo Olympics in 2021

Watching back in the United States, Lee's family leapt with joy. Her father pumped his fist in the air from his wheelchair. "This medal means a lot to me because I just didn't think I would ever get here with the injuries," says Lee. "I'm super proud of myself for sticking with it."

>>> Lee shows love for her family, friends, and country after her floor routine.

Lee had already made history as the first Hmong-American gymnast. Now, she was the first Hmong-American Olympic gold medalist. She was also the sixth American woman to take gold in the all-around. Lee took bronze in the uneven bars. The U.S. team received the silver medal. In her home state of Minnesota, Governor Tim Walz, made July 30th Sunisa Lee Day.

〉〉〉 Lee's family and friends celebrate her Olympic all-around win.

CHAPTER FIVE

COLLEGE LIFE AND BEYOND

After the Olympics, Lee started college as a freshman at Auburn University. Her coach's twin brother, Jeff Graba, coached there. Lee had decided to go to Auburn as a young teen. For the past five years, she'd been coming to the campus to visit coach Graba and train.

After high school, Lee officially joined the Auburn gymnastics team. "I really just wanted to come to college to try and find my love for the sport again," says Lee. "At the Olympics, it didn't really take it away, but leading up to that was super hard, so in my head, I didn't want to do it again. Here (Auburn) it's the complete opposite, just being able to have fun and not really worry about anything."

〉〉〉 Lee competes on the beam in the 2022 Division I Women Gymnastics Championship.

Lee also wanted to be part of a team to keep growing and developing as a gymnast. As an elite gymnast, she often trained and competed alone. "When you're an elite gymnast, it's so hard because you have to sacrifice so many things and you can't hang out with friends," says Lee. "So coming here it feels like a relief because I get to go out with my friends and like have fun. And the [gymnastics] team here is just amazing."

>>> Lee and her Auburn teammates are introduced to the fans before a competition.

>>> Lee and her Auburn teammates get pumped up before a competition.

Raising Awareness

While Lee went out with friends one evening, an attacker sprayed her with pepper spray. He also yelled racial slurs at her. After the incident, Lee used her celebrity status to speak out on hate crimes against Asian Americans and Pacific Islanders (AAPI). According to the group Stop AAPI Hate, hate crimes rose since the COVID-19 pandemic. The group receives reports and educates communities on hate crimes.

Lee continued to make history during her first year competing at the college level. In a 2022 meet, Lee became the first gymnast on a college team to perform the Nabieva skill on the uneven bars. This skill is one of the most difficult skills to perform. Lee laid **vertically** over the high bar. She swung around and passed over the bar backwards before grabbing it again. It was the same move that helped her win the gold medal in Tokyo. Later, Lee performed a stunning routine on the balance beam. She scored her first perfect 10 of the season for that routine! She was the first Auburn gymnast to score a 10 in their home arena.

Lee also helped her team to a fourth-place finish by the end of the season. It was Auburn's best ranking in the history of the program. Lee announced that she would be returning to the team for the 2022–23 season.

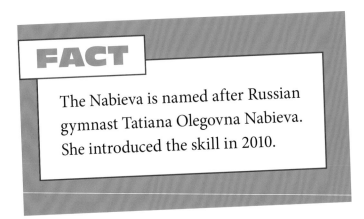

FACT

The Nabieva is named after Russian gymnast Tatiana Olegovna Nabieva. She introduced the skill in 2010.

>>> Lee won the 2022 NCAA National Championship on the balance beam.

With all its ups and downs, Lee's gymnastics journey continues to inspire others. In 2021, *TIME* magazine named Lee one of the 100 most **influential** people of the year. Five-time medalist Nastia Liukin wrote, "Suni has an impact that extends far beyond any border or sport. This milestone sends a simple yet powerful message to underrepresented people everywhere: Dream big because anything is possible."

〉〉〉 Lee throws out the first pitch at a Minnesota Twins game.

TIMELINE

2003   Sunisa Phabsomphou Lee is born on March 9, 2003, in St. Paul, Minnesota.

2009   Lee starts gymnastics at Midwest Gymnastics in Little Canada, Minnesota.

2010   Lee wins her first all-around at a state meet.

2012   Lee performs a gold-medal Olympic-level move on the beam.

2016   Lee debuts as an elite gymnast at the U.S. Classic.

2017   Lee is invited to join the U.S. National Team.

2019   Lee places first in the uneven bars, second in the all-around, and third in the floor routine at the U.S. National Championships.

2019   Lee wins the silver medal for her floor routine and bronze medal for the uneven bars at the World Championships.

2021   Lee wins the all-around gold medal, team silver medal, and uneven bars bronze medal at the Tokyo Olympics.

2021   Lee starts college at Auburn University and joins the gymnastics team.

2022   Lee makes history becoming the first collegiate gymnast to perform the Nabieva on the uneven bars.

GLOSSARY

COVID-19 (KOH-vid nine-TEEN)—a very contagious and sometimes deadly virus that spread worldwide in 2020

DEBUT (day-BYOO)—first public appearance

ELITE (uh-LEET)—a group of people whose skills are higher than others

FRONT AERIAL (FRUHNT AYR-ee-uhl)—an acrobatic move in which a person completes a forward rotation of the body without touching the floor

HANDSPRING (HAND-spring)—an acrobatic move in which a person starts and lands in the upright position with a handstand in the middle

IMMIGRATE (IM-uh-grayt)—coming to live permanently in another country

INFLUENTIAL (in-floo-EN-chuhl)—to affect or change in an important way

PARALYZED (PARE-uh-lyzed)—unable to move all or part of the body

REFUGEE (re-fyoo-JEE)—a person forced to leave their country to escape danger

VERTICAL (VUR-tuh-kuhl)—upright

READ MORE

Fishman, John M. *Suni Lee*. Minneapolis: Lerner Publications, 2022.

Simons, Lisa M. Bolt. *Simone Biles: Gymnastics Legend*. Mankato, MN. Capstone Press, 2021.

Walduck, Vincent. *My Book of Gymnastics*. London, UK: DK Publishing, 2020.

INTERNET SITES

DK Find Out! Gymnastics
dkfindout.com/us/sports/gymnastics/

Olympic Gymnastics Website
olympics.com/ioc/international-gymnastics-federation

The Gymternet
thegymter.net

INDEX

AUTHOR BIO

Cheryl Kim is an elementary school teacher from California currently teaching at an international school in Thailand. She lives in Chiang Mai with her husband Brandon and sons Nathanael and Zachary.